THE
ABUNDANT
LIFE

A Biblical Approach

By

E. G. Sherman, Jr. Ph.D.

i

THE ABUNDANT LIFE

Cover designed by Dominion Multi-media
Tallahassee, Florida
Editor - The Late Dr. Brenda E. Powell

DG PUBLISHING HOUSE
Lake Park, GA
850-728-0815

ACKNOWLEDGMENT

This book grew out of the author's extensive professional experiences as a University Professor, an active pastor, and an academic dean of a Bible College and Seminary. His academic specialties include: sociology, gerontology, death and dying, history and philosophy - all anchored him for a long tenure in both the academic and religious arenas. Within both professional settings, the author found a common human desire; it was that of quest for abundance ranging from finance to friendship. Unfortunately, many of the individuals focused on abundance without a clear perception of its acquisition and utilization.

The author, in this connection, used both the classroom and the pulpit to instill a practical and ethical approach for the quest of abundance. Based upon the numerous reports from students and parishioners, the admonitions and guidelines have been of great value. In grateful appreciation for those reports with the positive feedback, this book is being dedicated to those believers. Additionally, it is an expression of gratitude to my late wife (2008) Dr. Dolores E. Sherman, who endured the protracted time periods of listening to the oral reading as this manuscript was being prepared for publication. Lastly, words of thanks and appreciation are conveyed to the late (2011) Dr. Brenda E. Powell, head of the English Department at Monroe Comprehensive High School, for her editorial assistance.

The Abundant Life denotes one's perception of personal fulfillment in the physical, social, economic, and spiritual arenas. Although it does include a heavy emphasis on materialism, the abundant life is more focused on self image rather than the quality or quantity of abundant indicators that one possesses. Further, views of the abundant life vary with factors that include age, race, gender, residence, socioeconomic status, education and family back ground.

Additionally, the great "economic divide" causes variations in what is viewed as The Abundant Life; yet, every person has some desire to experience The Abundant Life. Accordingly, this book has been prepared to give a spiritual view of The Abundant Life and how to attain it.

Table of Contents

Preface

Numerous are the books, cassettes, tapes, CD's, and DVD's on attaining the abundant life. The themes or approaches range from a secular to a religious orientation. Within the secular approaches are psychological, counseling, self help therapies, and "fortune tellers." The sacred (religious) orientation, in contrast, relies on teachings embedded in sacred books, doctrines, and creeds. The religious approach varies in orientation, theological foundation, faith groups, and contents.

The Judeo-Christian religion as practiced in America encourages and sanctions economic prosperity as reflected in the "Rags to Riches" Saga. However, the evolution of this country failed to allow all inhabitants an opportunity to attain affluence. Ironically, both groups developed a reliance on religion to cope with their status in life: one extended praises for its blessings while the other offered petitions for its improvement. Hence, each group embraced the lofty ideal of the abundant life.

The Holy Bible has many teachings on the reality of living, one of which is the abundant life. Since this theme encompasses many facets of living beyond mere economics, this volume was prepared to offer a biblical excursion on the pathway to the abundant life. Its approach was to integrate the theological, sociological, historical, and psychological orientations into a practical set of guidelines for sermons. Its guiding objective was to enrich the reader's knowledge of the Judeo Christian religious teaching on the abundant life with no latent purpose of persuasion to accept a particular faith or denominational position.

Eugene G. Sherman, Jr. was born in Whigham, Georgia in 1932. He has earned the B.A., M.A., Ph.D., D.S.T., Degrees along with the honorary Doctor of Divinity and Doctor of Humanities and Letters. His professional experiences have included forty years of University teaching in sociology, history, philosophy, gerontology, and history. He was awarded the title of Emeritus Professor of Sociology (2002) by Albany State University, Albany, Georgia. Within those four decades in academe, the author published numerous funded proposals. He was also active in two areas of the religious arena: Pastor of The Institutional First Baptist Church in Albany, Georgia since 1971 and Academic Dean of Bethany Divinity College and Seminary in Dothan, Alabama from 1988 until June 2011 when he retired.

INTRODUCTION

Abundance is a topic found in both Testaments of the Bible. It appears early in Genesis, is especially prominent in the Poetic Books, is mentioned by some of the Prophets, and is widely used in the New Testament. The ministry of Jesus included references to and demonstrations of abundance. On one occasion, Jesus said of his mission, "I am come that they might have life and have it more abundantly" (John 10:10).

During his ministry of approximately three and one half years, Jesus demonstrated abundance in many aspects of human life. He provided food for five thousand persons, he restored sight to a blind man, he healed the ten lepers, he freed the man with demonic spirits, and he raised Lazarus from the dead.

Much has been written about the life and ministry of Jesus and as one biblical writer, John, noted, "And there are also many other things which Jesus did, the which, if they should be written everyone, I suppose that even the world itself could not contain the books that should be written. Amen."

Admittedly, John was writing prior to the invention of the printing press and Centuries before the telecommunication network. It should be noted, however, that no attempt is herein made in this book to evaluate or criticize the scope of Jesus' teachings and works nor the volumes required to record his activities.

Instead, the emphasis is placed on providing guidelines for use by those who desire to experience the abundant life that Jesus promised. These guidelines are biblically anchored and they have been organized under nine different aspects of abundance within this manuscript.

This book makes no claim to enhance economic abundance; its intent is, rather, to inspire the reader to strive for a holistic self-image that encompasses happiness, self actualization, optimism, and contentment. Hopefully, such a positive self image will help the reader to experience <u>The Abundant Life.</u>

CHAPTER 1

The Abundant Life: Its Source (God)
The Divine Creator
Genesis 1, 2, 3:1-3, Psalm 8

One of the historic mysteries is that of the beginning of the world and all forms of human life. Explanations of the beginnings, while numerous and varied in contents, can be reduced to two views: namely, Creation and Evolution. Each of these perspectives is rooted in a body of knowledge. Creation relies on the Bible for its account of the beginning. Further, it depicts God as the source of creation. Hence, the Bible asserts -" In the beginning God created the heaven and the earth." (Genesis 1:1). The opposing view, Evolution, is based upon scientific knowledge and it avers that a "great bang" occurrence gave rise to the earth and the humankind evolved from a lower form of animal life.

These two views have been the nexus of widespread discussion in academic, religious, and lay settings. The intensity of this controversy reached national prominence in a court case labeled as the "Monkey Trial." The defendant, Scope, was accused of teaching evolution in the classroom. The court found him guilty but issued no harsh

The Abundant Life: Its Source (God)

Sentence.

Without attempting to decry Evolution, the focus of this writing is to present the Creation Theory as the first cause of the solar system and all forms of life. This stance is biblically supported and impenetrable by the scientific inquiry. The writing, in this connection, will be undergirded by three proposition regarding God as maker, namely: God is the source of creation; God made provisions for humankind; and God is the final judge.

To enrich the appreciation of God's action much beyond the three delineated areas, attention will be focused on the word, God. Although the concept, God, extends beyond the ability of humanity to comprehend, it has been fitted into an area of study known as Systematic Theology. This area focuses more on the attributes - features assigned to God - than the intrinsic nature of God. Such a restriction is unavoidable because the use of human language is totally inadequate to fully describe the origin and nature of God. Therefore, it must be concluded that human views of God are structured by language, geographical area, teachings, and personal experiences.

Accordingly, there are widespread differences among people with respect to their view of God, request of God, dependency on God, and trust in God. This fact leads to the earlier defined propositions regarding God as used in this writing, the first of which is - God is the source of creation. It is a truism that

The Abundant Life: Its Source (God)

humanity from primitive to contemporary times has recognized that some power was responsible for creating the world and its various forms of life. The Judeo Christian embraced the notion that this origin must be traced back to God.

Hence, Christians accept the biblical explanation of creation as found in Genesis 1:1. Therein the Bible states, "In the beginning God created the heaven and the earth." Beloved, this creative process extended over a period of six days, it was progressive, exact, and good (Genesis 1:31). Attesting to the efficiency of God's creative actions, according to (Ps. 19:1) "The heavens declare(d) the glory of God and the firmament sheweth his handiwork." These creative acts of God were manifestations of his ability, control,

The Abundant Life: Its Source (God)

and ownership. The Psalmist was fully aware of this divine prerogative as reflected in the words, "The earth is the Lord's and they that dwell therein" (Psalm 24:1).

In this regard, there are no scarcities in the products of God's creation; instead, there was and continues to be <u>abundance of divine provisions.</u> To have dominion over the earthly parts of his provisions, God created man (Genesis 2:7). He placed Adam as the first federal head of the divine provisions. Since the time of Adam the utilization, allocation, and control of these provisions have been under humankind. The reality of this assertion leads to the second proposition which is - God made provisions for humanity.

The Abundant Life: Its Source (God)

These creative acts existed on two levels: physical and spiritual. Because God felt that there would be unity between himself and human kind, his first act for humanity was to provide for the physical need. The Psalmist, in writing of this priority noted, " What is man, that thou art mindful of him? and the son of man that thou visitest him? For thou hast made him a little lower than the angels, and hast crowned him with glory and honor. Thou hast made him to have dominion over the works of thy hands: thou hast put all things under his feet..." (Psalm 8:4-6).

Beloved, this Scripture is a clear indication of divine abundance so any scarcities are humanly created, whether by social codes or a lack of personal efforts.

The second level of divine provision was in the spiritual realm. In the initial relations between the first family (Adam and Eve), there was perfect harmony. The couple enjoyed fellowship with God, but it had also received an order to avoid eating from the tree of knowledge. A violation of that divine order would bring about a break in the unity between it and God.

In the meantime, God had equipped the couple with free will. However, it would be held accountable for the improper use of that capacity (Genesis 2:16-17). Sadly, the couple transgressed the order and it was expelled from the Garden of Eden. That expulsion created a void between the couple and God.

The Abundant Life: Its Source (God)

However, God - the merciful being - allowed its descendants to engage in many rituals and sacrifices in an effort to reestablish the divine union with the Heavenly Father. So in the process of time, God sent forth his son to reunite the broken chain between Himself and humanity. Saint John described the rationale for the birth of Jesus by noting, "For God so loved the world that He gave His only begotten Son that whosoever believeth in Him should not perish but have everlasting life" (John 3:16).

My friends, this divine act was the expression of God's mercy in opening the way by which the spiritual reunion, by personal choice, could be reestablished. In writing about the purpose of Jesus' birth, John noted, "For God sent not his Son into

The Abundant Life: Its Source (God)

the world to condemn the world: but that the world through Him might be saved". (John 3:17). These two verses contain adequate proof for the assertion that God offers spiritual provisions for anyone who is willing to believe in the finished work of Jesus (Romans 10:9). The prospect of assessing this spiritual provision will last until the Second Coming of Christ, a period also known as the Rapture. It will be followed by a subsequent judgment in Heaven. The certainty of this fact leads to the third, and final proposition of this writing on God as the source of the abundant life; namely, God is the Eternal Judge.

The problems of living included many disappointments, injustices, and grief. However, the Bible calls upon believers to "Fret not thyself because of evil doers, neither be thou envious against workers of iniquity. For they shall soon be cut down like grass, and wither as the green herb" (Psalm 37:1-2) It also encourages us to show restraint in dealing with adversaries and leave the ultimate outcome to God. "Vengeance is mine, saith the Lord and whatsoever is right that will I repay, saith the Lord" (Romans 12:19). Friends, these and many other Scriptures call upon us to exercise rigorous self-control as we move along this pathway of life. They also remind us that there will come a time when all must stand before the judgment seat of God.

At that time all acts of omission and commission will be put on display and reward for the righteous will be given

The Abundant Life: Its Source (God)

while punishment for the unrighteous will be imposed. (Rev.20:12-15).

So in closing, dear believers, this writing has shown that God is the source of the abundant life. It briefly skimmed the surface of Theology in commenting on God. Let us remember, however, that God extends beyond the human mind to adequately describe or fully understand. As an alternative to a complete comprehension of God, we believers embrace the following attributes of God, namely: all knowing, all powerful, everywhere present, and forever unchangeable. Therefore we should take comfort in the knowledge that our abundance or lack of the same occurs under the watchful and compassionate eyes of the "Everlasting God" (Psalm 90:1). So as we seek to experience the Abundant Life, let us remember that God is the source; Jesus is our Advocate; The Holy Spirit is our energizer; Prayer is our channel; Faith is our anchor, and Righteous living is our obligation. Amen.

CHAPTER 2The Abundant Life: Its Reference (The Bible)
The Book of Books *2nd Timothy 2:15, 3:16*

There are billions of books in the world. This vast accumulation is the product of the printing. The books are largely kept in libraries; however, many are maintained in small offices, personal studies, publishing houses, and retail stores.

The books, also called resources, can be placed into two broad categories: namely, secular or worldly and sacred or religious. The secular books include history, geography, dictionaries and novels. In contrast, the sacred books include hymnals, Bibles, biblical commentaries, and Bible Dictionaries.

While both categories contain important and influential books, the Bible stands alone as the Book of Books. In view of the Bible's preeminence among books and the human need to know more about it, this chapter has been planned to investigate some features of this sacred document. Accordingly, it is entitled **The Book of Books.** The study will include three topics: namely, nature of the Bible, some values of its message, and some dangers in neglecting to study the Bible.

Prior to addressing these objectives, brief attention will be given to some historical views of the Bible. Probably no single source is more representation of public views than Halley's <u>Handbook of the Bible.</u> Hence, a partial listing of those views is herein cited. Abraham Lincoln wrote, "I believe the Bible is the best gift God has ever given to man".

Daniel Webster penned, "If there is anything in my thoughts or style to commend, the credit is due to my parents for instilling in me the early love of the Scriptures." Patrick Henry asserted, "The Bible is worth all other books which have ever been printed." Charles Dickens submitted, "The New Testament is the very best book that ever was or ever will be known in the world" and, Immanuel Kant insisted, "The existence of the Bible, as a book for the people, is the greatest benefit which the human race has ever experienced.

The Abundant Life: Its Source (God)

Shifting from these views of the Bible, let us now turn to the earlier specified topics, the first of which is - the nature of the Bible. This line of inquiry focuses on the question as to the essence of the Bible, or its origin, contents, and duration. The word, Bible, comes from the Greek Word, Biblio, a word that denotes a collection of holy scripts.   The Bible consists of 66 Books: 37 of which constitute the Old Testament and the remaining 27 comprise the New Testament. The Bible is the history of God's sovereign power and ultimate plan for the universe.   The Bible, often referred to as the Word, was authored by God - but recorded by man. This fact is found in the 2nd Peter 1:21 where it is recorded, "For the prophecy came not in old time by the will of man: but holy men of God spake as they were moved by the Holy Ghost."

The Old Testament division of the Bible was written by The Emancipator, Moses, Kings, Prophets, a Builder, and Priests. In contrast, the New Testament writers were earlier disciples and later Apostles. The Bible, notwithstanding its lengthy history, has withstood critical inquiries regarding its factual basis. No attempt will be made herein to exhaust the list of archeological findings that have supported biblical assertions. However, a passing reference will be made to three findings that are consistent with biblical teachings. The first is that of Noah's ark; Archeologist found the wreckage of a vessel in the land of Turkey that conforms

The Abundant Life: Its Source (God)

to the biblical account of that ark. Secondly, there was a finding of Old Testament scrolls in a cave in 1948. That discovery is also known as the Dead Sea scrolls. Friends, it dates back to the Old Testament period and, interestingly, the same books therein are those found in the King James Version of the Bible. Lastly, two years ago Archeologists, in Jerusalem, uncovered a burial site that contained a grave marked, James the son of Mary and the brother of Jesus and Jude. Beloved, these three and many additional findings all support the claim of Apologetics - the aspect of theology that declares the Bible to be inerrant, infallible, and eternal.

Let us now turn to the second topic of this chapter; it is that of identifying some values of the Bible. As earlier indicated in the views on the Bible, it is valuable for moral instruction, spiritual precepts, general reading, and learning of God's creative, sustaining, and everlasting powers. The Bible is, further, valuable for documentation of prophecies and fulfillment, including the birth of Jesus and the ultimate Great White Throne judgment. The Apostle Paul dealt extensively on the value of the Bible. He complimented Timothy for his childhood reading of the Bible. Thus, Paul said to him, "From a child thou hast known the Holy Scriptures, which are able to make thee wise unto salvation through faith which is in Christ Jesus" (2nd Timothy 3:15). The next two verses of that same chapter provide additional support for the value of the Bible. Paul wrote, "All

The Abundant Life: Its Source (God)

scripture is given by the inspiration of God, and is profitable for doctrine, for reproof, for correction, for instruction in righteousness - that the man of God may be perfect, thoroughly furnished unto all good works".   (2nd Timothy 3:16-17).

The Bible's value is also found in its speaking to humanity regarding the problems of living, the prevalence of disappointments, the pains of illness, the grief of death, the confinement of infirmities, and the threshold of death. Certainly, these life realities cause us to shudder and grow sick at heart, but this same Bible contains messages of hope, blessed assurance, and the eternal promise of everlasting life for all who accept the finished work of Jesus Christ on the Cross at Calvary.   With this

The Abundant Life: Its Source (God)

wonderful list of values to be derived from the Bible, attention will now be turned to the last objective of this chapter; it is that of <u>citing some dangers in neglecting to study the Bible.</u>

No pilot would attempt an international flight without having a flight plan; no condo builder would attempt any construction without have a set of blueprints; no extensive land traveler would commence a trip without a map; nor would a commercial chef try new dishes without a collection of recipes. In a like manner, any serious and believing Christian must have the document, or road map, that points to everlasting life. The Holy Bible, in this connection, is the document that God provided for humanity to use on its sojourn called life. Just as there are dangers in failing to have a flight plan, blueprints, recipes, and road maps - there are more soul threatening dangers in neglecting to have, use, and believe in the Bible. The magnitude of these dangers is a recurring theme in the Bible. Let us, at this time, take a look at some of the dangers or pitfalls:

<u>Materialism</u> - This is the over zealous attempt to become rich, but the Bible warns, "What has a person to profit if he gains the world and loses his soul?" (Mark 8:36).

<u>Vengeance</u> - Often daily life encompasses unfair treatments being imposed by mean spirited persons, but the Bible assures victims that, "Vengeance is mine; I will repay, saith the Lord." (Romans 12:19).

<u>Illness</u> - Many are the people who

suffer prolonged illness, but the Bible calls upon such individuals to remember the faith of Job who said, "...All the days of my appointed time will I wait, till my change come."(Job 14:14).

In addition to these pitfalls aggravated by neglecting to reading the Bible, there are two other critical areas where Biblical knowledge is needed; they are the Christian's spiritual dress and the Christian's spiritual stance. Saint Paul addressed both of these areas. The first is found in Ephesians 6:10-17 where he calls upon Christians to "Put on the whole armor of God, that ye may be able to stand against the wiles of the devil." Saint Paul's second warning against neglecting to read the Bible is found in 2nd Timothy 4:3-4 where he predicted "...the time will come when they will not endure sound doctrine; but after their own lusts shall they heap to themselves teachers, having itching ears; And they shall turn away their ears from the truth, and shall be turned into fables."

So, in closing this chapter on The Abundant Life: Its Reference: (The Bible), let us remember that the Bible is The Book of Books. We should, therefore, never take lightly this Book because -as Christians, we accept it as The Word of God. This Book has withstood the test of time; its message is perpetual; its contents infallible; its purpose is divine. Hence, the Bible - symbolically, is our bridge over troubled waters; shelter in the storms of life; the key to <u>the storehouse to God's abundances </u>and the roadmap to eternal existence with the Father. Can we believe it? Well if we believe in Jesus, we can safely believe in the Bible because Jesus said, "Heaven and earth shall pass away: but my word shall not pass away." (Luke 21:33).

Having read this chapter on the Book of Books, hopefully, you have gleaned insights on the divine reference for attaining the Abundant Life. Remember, it is merely believing in messages contained in the Bible. With this anchor, you are ready to pursue the chapters that follow on The <u>Abundant Life</u>, which understood and embraced, will lead to The Abundant Life.

The Abundant Life: Its Source (God)

CHAPTER 3 The Abundant Life: Its Access (Jesus)

The Abundant Life

"... I am come that they may have life, and have it more abundantly." John 10:10

It is generally known that humanity has a need for the economic necessities of life; this need includes food, clothing and shelter. While existing throughout the history of civilization, these economic needs have been met by various human efforts. Starting at the hunting and fishing stage, humankind has evolved to a modern technological system for

The Abundant Life: Its Access (Jesus)

supplying economic needs. The unfortunate fact, however, is that access to the supplies are hampered by limited to even no income to make the necessary are purchases. At the other extreme, those individuals who are blessed with an abundance of economic goods. In view of this twofold division of humankind in the economic sphere, writing has been entitled," The Abundant Life". It will be anchored in one of the purposes of Jesus' earthly sojourn - that of promoting the abundant life; however, it will specify three biblical requirements that we must meet in order to experience the abundant life. They are: to accept Jesus as Lord and Savior; follow the prayer model that Jesus gave; and to cast your cares upon him. As noted in these three requirements, one's preparation for the abundant life must be anchored in a spiritual view of life. The Scriptures are filled with teachings on both the pros and cons of efforts to attain the abundant life.

Prior to exploring the three earlier specified requirements for obtaining the abundant life, attention will be focused on the Americans' fascination with the abundant life. Over one hundred and fifty years ago, a French writer noted that Americans are more concerned with material things than with ethics, morality, and religion. He was correct as reflected in the notion of "rags to riches", "upward mobility", and keeping up with the Joneses. From the time of that writing up to the present age, Americans have been preoccupied with moving up in society.

The Abundant Life: Its Access (Jesus)

We are frequently overworked, over obligated, and over committed to organizations - all in an effort to satisfy our urge for material success. Beloved, this writing is no condemnation of material success, but it does signal a warning against total involvement with material gains. Remember, the Bible raises the question, "For what shall it profit a man if he shall gain the whole world, and lose his soul" (Mark 8:37). Within this question, Jesus is not condemning prosperity for his promised access to the abundant life. The important question, thus becomes, what is the abundant life?   It is one of having access to funds beyond mere day-to-day survival; to having health, soundness of mind, and a general satisfaction with self.

Having defined the abundant life, attention will now be focused on the three earlier specified requirements for experiencing the abundant life, the first of which is - to accept Jesus as Lord and Savior. Beloved the Bible tells us that "For God so loved the world, that he gave His only begotten Son that whosoever believeth in Him should not perish, but have everlasting life" (John 3:16). In addition to providing the pathway for eternal existence with the Heavenly Father, Jesus also came in the role of the Shepherd. Thus, he said of himself, "I am the good shepherd: the good shepherd layeth down his life for his sheep" (John 10:11). These two Scriptures assure us that Jesus is concerned about our earthly experiences and our ultimate dwelling with the Father who is in heaven. However, of particular concern in this writing is the earthly provisions Jesus makes for our earthly abundance. In this regard, Jesus referred to himself not as just a shepherd, but as the Good Shepherd. This personal designation of himself with the words, I am, is used in several different contexts; thus, he said "I am the door, I am the light, I am the living water, I am the way, I am the bread, and I am the resurrection and the life." While all of these designations are essential for spiritual welfare, Jesus also referred to himself as the Good Shepherd. This reference was rooted in the sacrifice that the shepherd would make for the welfare of his sheep. Thus, Jesus said, "The good shepherd giveth his life for his sheep." His later death on Calvary attested to the sincerity of the Master's commitment to the sheep. Beloved, it was through that sacrificial death that Jesus - The Good

The Abundant Life: Its Access (Jesus)

Shepherd - rescued fallen humanity from the grip of sin.

    While each of the "I am" statements

is important, the Good Shepherd in my judgment, is the most valuable. In support of this conclusion, attention is called to the fact that the physical door can remain shut and it has no feeling about those who pass through; the physical bread provides strength but no thrust to salvation; and the earthly water is valuable for survival but it is incapable for personal atonement. But, beloved, I am so glad that The Good Shepherd conveys a completely different meaning. It refers to one whose compassion, commitment, and altruism were freely manifested in order that believers can experience the abundant life. This glorious fact leads to the second sub topic of this writing, which is knowing and

The Abundant Life: Its Access (Jesus)

believing in the twofold prayer model that Jesus gave. Beloved, the first aspect of Jesus' prayer model is noted in Matthew 6:9-15. Within that prayer is found: to whom prayer should be address, for what the petitioner is requesting, and a recognition of the everlasting existence of the Heavenly Father.

The next aspect of Jesus' teaching on prayer is focused on how the believer should express his desires. Jesus' instruction was for the petitioner to ask of the Father in his name; to ask believing that he has received and he shall receive, and to avoid babbling as the heathens. (Matthew 6:7) In summary, the method for prayer is that of recognition, petitioning, and believing.

Thirdly, the final requirement in preparing for the abundance is to cast all our cares upon the Lord. (1st Peter 5:7) In this teaching, Peter was referring to the certainty of problems occurring during our journey. His recommendation was to avoid, "Shuddering and growing sick at heart" but rather turn the situation over to Jesus as Lord and Savior. In a slightly different context, Jesus offered a solution to the exhaustive problems of living. He summoned believers to "Come unto me, all ye that labor and are heavily laden, and I will give you rest." (Matthew 11:28). The teachings of both Jesus and Peter address a widespread experience of many people, including dedicated believers. It just seems that life, for many persons, contains many unanticipated experiences, one of which is a scarcity or inaccessibility of resources that will enhance the quality of living. Hence, many are the individuals who yearn to share in the abundant life.

In closing, this writing was entitled, "The Abundant Life". It was based upon a teaching of Jesus; he said that he came in order for us to have life and have it more abundantly. If we are to enjoy the abundant life, we must accept Jesus as Lord and Savior, follow his prayer model and cast all our cares upon him. Finally, may the Good Lord Bless and Keep you during your earthly sojourn and own you at the Great White Throne of Judgment.

CHAPTER 4

The Abundant Life: Its Divine Thrust (Prayer) Prayer in Action

1st Timothy 2:1 and Romans 8:15-16, 26-27

All traditional religions include a process for communing with their Supreme Being. In the Christian Religion, that process is known as prayer. While Christianity has no monopoly on prayer, it does stand alone as the religion whose founder taught his disciples how to pray and was, by the power of God, raised from the dead.

Prayer is a recurring theme in both testaments of the Bible. In the Old

The Abundant Life: Its Divine Thrust
(Prayer)

Testament, however, prayer was focused largely on the welfare of Israel whereas the New Testament prayer emphasis is on the individual's earthly sojourn and ultimate outcome at the judgment seat of God. This writing, in this connection, was planned to examine prayer as a process and as a focus. It has been entitled, "Prayer in Action". The writing includes three windows of inquiry, namely 1) how we should pray, 2) why we should pray, and 3) for whom should we pray.

Since this is the last of a three part series on prayer and background information was earlier presented, this writing today will omit a section on history and move to the earlier stated inquiries - the first of which is <u>how should</u>

The Abundant Life: Its Divine Thrust
(Prayer)

we pray? Both Jesus and Saint Paul addressed the question of how should we pray? Jesus gave a prayer model (Matthew 6:11) of what we should include in our prayer. As noted in Matthew 6:5, Jesus placed humility above vanity; thus, He labeled as hypocrites those persons who loved to pray in public for the praises of people. With in that same Scripture, Jesus emphasized sincerity and the ability to believe as ingredients of prayer. Accordingly, He said that we should shut out the world and enter in our secret closet for prayer. Within that prayerful mood, we must rise to the level of believing that we have received before the actuality occurs.

Saint Paul, in several of his letters, dealt with the matter of how we should pray. He admonished the Ephesians to

*The Abundant Life: Its Divine Thrust
(Prayer)*

pray always with all prayer and supplication in the Spirit. Paul knew that the Spirit gives power to the words of prayer because the Bible teaches that the Spirit groans on our behalf.

Paul's theme on how to pray was

also included in his letter to the Philippians wherein he admonished them to be careful for nothing; but in everything by prayer and supplications with thanksgiving let your request be made known unto God (Phil 4:6). Having explored some aspects of how we should pray, let us now turn to the second consideration which is Why should we pray?

The Holy Bible has numerous

reasons as to why we should pray. Probably, the most pervasive reason is that God repeatedly commanded that we should pray. (1st Samuel 12:23 and Romans 12:12). Secondly, we should pray to follow the example of our Lord and Savior Jesus; he taught the disciples how to pray and he gave instruction as to how humanity should pray. We should, further, pray because it is a sure method to defeat the devil, our great adversary. (1st Peter 4:7) We should, further, pray to discern the will of God (Luke 11:9-10). Although there are countless other reasons for our prayer, we should especially pray to adore God, to thank God, to beseech God, to stay ready to meet God.

The last consideration in our

The Abundant Life: Its Divine Thrust
(Prayer)

writing is that of for whom should we pray? Although it may seem egotistic, the fact remains that we should first pray for ourselves. Peter prayed to the Lord as he began to sink," Lord Save Me". The dying thief prayed to Jesus, "Lord when thou cometh into thy kingdom remember me". Luke tells of two men going up to pray for themselves; one was a Pharisee and the other was a Publican. (Luke 18:9-17). While each was praying for himself, there was a marked contrast in how they presented themselves in prayer. The Pharisee was egoistic, somewhat boastful and recounted his life of fasting and giving of tithes. The Publican was less boastful and, instead, stood afar off while not lifting up..." his eyes unto heaven, but smote upon his breast, saying, God be merciful to me a sinner". Both of the men received a divine response, but only the Publican was justified. Implicit in this Scriptural account is the fact that we must approach the throne of Grace in humility and them spread our wants before His face.   In so doing, we must never forget that Jesus said, **"Fear not, little flock; for it is your Father's good pleasure to give you the kingdom" (Luke 12:32).**Herein is one secret to **The Abundant Life.**

Our second level of prayer should be for one another.   James 5:16 calls upon us to, "Confess your faults one to another, and pray one for another, that ye may be healed."   This act of praying one for another was a practice of Saint Paul; thus, he told the Romans "... without ceasing I make mention of you always in my prayers." (Romans 1: 9).   The matter of praying for others was also addressed in the prayer model that Jesus taught. He instructed the disciples to say, "And forgive us our debts, as we forgive our debtors" (Matthew 6:12). Implicit in this request is the desire for a spiritual cleansing to unblock animosities that can block the flow of abundance in our life. Years earlier, the Psalmist gave a warning about negative feelings toward adversaries while craving the abundant life. He called upon the praying person to "Fret not thyself because of evil doers, neither be thou envious against workers of iniquity. For they shall soon be cut down like green herb." (Psalm 37:1-2).

We should, thirdly, pray for the less

The Abundant Life: Its Divine Thrust
(Prayer)

fortunate individuals. This prayer should be augmented with action in accordance with our resources. Jesus, in Matthew 25, gave a parable to illustrate the significance of stewardship. He talked about the Second Coming at which time one segment of would hear the words "Come ye blessed of my Father's house" while the other would be sent away into everlasting punishment. (Matthew 21:31-40) In sum, the only difference between the sheep and goats was in their actions toward the less fortunate. The challenge, in this connection, is for humankind to not only pray for the less fortunate, but to render aid whenever possible. In so doing, such individuals will be anchoring themselves to experience the abundant life.

The Abundant Life: Its Divine Thrust (Prayer)

Finally, the Bible tells us that we should pray for the sick. The Apostle James, half brother of Jesus, wrote, "Is any sick among you? Let him call for the elders of the church; and let them pray over him, anointing him with oil in the name of the Lord." (James 5:14-15). While prayer is potent, it must be noted that medical technology is an asset in sickness and should never be excluded for total reliance on prayer while seeking the abundant life.

In closing, we have looked at prayer in action - a subject that denotes movement. This writing has sought to illustrate that prayer is more than a poem or a speech to be uttered. It is rather a humble approach to the throne of God, driven by an unalterable faith that God answers prayer and makes possible for one to experience the abundant life.

CHAPTER 5

The Abundant Life: Its Prerequisite (Faith) Faith In Stormy Times

1st Kings 19:2-3 "Then Jezebel sent a messenger unto Elijah, saying, So let the gods do to me, and more also, if I make not thy life as the life of one of them by to-morrow about this time".

The experiences of life are numerous and diversified. Some are pleasant, but many are unpleasant; some are short in duration, but others are protracted; some promote tranquility, but others cause unrest; and some progressive, but others are short lived. Yet, life for the most part is a reality that includes good and bad times.

Since humanity tends to prefer the gratifying experiences of life, it tends to follow that extended disappointing experiences cause hurt, anger, and anxiety. The pervasiveness of disappointing life experiences lead to a condition known as mental storms. This handwriting, in this connection, has been planned to examine mental storms and to recommend the Biblical method for weathering the storms of life. It will be herein submitted that Faith is the requirement for coping with the storms of life. Hence, the writing has been entitled, "Faith in Stormy Times". This writing will be undergirded by the following three objectives: namely, to identify and discourage passive responses; to specify and encourage active responses; and to recommend "Faith" as the means to cope with the stormy times of life. As noted in the earlier reading, the textual base of this writing was lifted from the 1st Kings, Chapter 19, verses 2 and 3. Within that recording is the account of a Major Prophet, Elijah, who - after having earlier been the instrument of God's power - now stands amidst stormy times.

A brief profile will be given as part of the background for this writing. However, two concepts will precede this narrative; the words are faith and stormy. Our Bible defines faith in Hebrews 11:1 as "the substance of things hoped for, the evidence of things not seen." The next word, storm, denotes a disturbance of the atmosphere; it is usually overwhelming and even destructive. The storm can assume a variety of forms, each of which

The Abundant Life: Its Prerequisite (Faith)

has its special features; some of the storms are: rain accompanied by a drenching downpour of water; wind causing a turbulent gush of atmospheric pressure; hail producing massive ice droplets; lightening associated with flashes of light and roaming thunder; dust that produces gushes of sand; and snow yielding massive piles of snow. While these and all other atmospheric disturbances can cause some disruption in human action, there is another more potent storm and, literally, feasts on the mental nature of people. It is referred to, in this writing, as the mental storm. Whereas proper clothing, shoes, and eye shades offer a safe measure against the atmospheric storms, they are all ineffective when one is facing the mental storms of life.

The Abundant Life: Its Prerequisite (Faith)

Friends, these mental storms are insidious; they are sneaky, they are progressive, they are powerful, they are dangerous, and they will ultimately conquer the victim unless early intervention is sought. Beloved, the sad fact is that so many people are besieged by these storms and, yet, they are in a state of denial. In the mean time, the condition is intensifying as time passes on.

Against this background on the concepts faith, storms, and mental storms, let us now take a quick look at Elijah - that great a prophet who found himself encountering mental storms. Elijah was a major prophet chosen by God to carry a message of condemnation to King Ahab and Jezebel. The King had allowed his people to shift loyalty from Jehovah to Baal. This apostasy was

The Abundant Life: Its Prerequisite (Faith)

displeasing to God. Thus, he instructed
Elijah to confront Ahab. Initially, the
King disregarded Elijah and viewed him as
a mere religious zealot. But God had a
method then, as does He now, to get
attention from even the hard-hearted
people. Thus, he instructed Elijah to tell
the King that there would be no rain until
he, Elijah, so ordered it. True to this
prophecy, no rain occurred until it was
ordered by Elijah. Next, Elijah called for
a contest between Baal and Jehovah.
The story is known of how Baal failed to
send down fire; in contrast, Elijah's God
send down fire and consumed the animal
offering, the wood. Next, Elijah slew the
prophets of Baal. That slaying was the
basis of Jezebel's message to Elijah; in it
she promised to take his life at about the
same time that he had a day earlier slain

the prophets of Baal. Friends, that message caused a mental storm in the life of Elijah. To briefly speculate - how is it that a powerful man such as Elijah could become victimized by mental storms? Had he forgotten the Jehovah who had earlier sent down a flame of fire from Heaven? Did Elijah think, instead, that he was the source of the fire? Was he unsure about God's ability to protect him, his messenger and prophet?

These questions lead to the earlier identified objectives, the first of which is to identify and discourage passive responses. Upon receiving the threat, Elijah arose and left the city; he later left his servant and went into the wilderness to hide from Jezebel's soldiers. There the great Prophet assumed the role of a wimp! There he uttered, "Oh, Lord, take away my life; for I am not better than my fathers." While there, Elijah was fed on cake and had water to drink, yet he was still torn by mental storms. But the Lord was still concerned by his prophet; hence, an angel was dispatched to take an active stance against his mental storms.

Friends, that divine experience did not completely remove Elijah's mental storms. Next, he went into a cave only to later hear the Lord ask why was he there. Again, Elijah's response was that of a complainer. He talked about how many followers Ahab had and that he was the only one who had not yielded to Ahab. The Lord reminded Elijah that he had hundred of prophets who had not so yielded to Ahab. The Lord's message to Elijah to get out of the cave leads to the second concern of this writing - that of taking a positive stand or seeking personal empowerment with respect to mental storms. Friends, when Elijah finally decided to heed God's message, he had begun the necessary treatment to cope with his mental storms. Notice in verses 11-13, the attentiveness that Elijah showed toward finding an indication of God. Those verses speak to us today; they tell us that we must set aside some quality time if we want to hear from and respond to God. This approach is known as the proactive approach; it means that we are attempting to help ourselves, but under the canopy of God's guidance.

The effective use of this approach leads to the final aspect of this writing today; it is that of recommending faith as the medicine, therapy, technique, or method for coping with the mental storms of life. Oh! There will be times when dark clouds rise, but remember that there will be a brighter day ahead. There will be times when arrows pierce your soul, but remember that there is a balm in Gilead. There will be times when billows roll against your soul, but remember that the winds and waves obey His will. Friends, in those desolate moments when we cannot seem to tunnel through to God's pipeline of mercy; times when we seem unable to feel the warmth of his spirit; times when scarcity in resources overwhelm us;. times when our tear soaked eyes can see nothing but trouble ahead - that is the time when we must begin to walk by faith and not by sight. That is the time when we, like Elijah, can find God in that still small voice; a time when we shall begin to experience

<u>abundance</u> and, lastly, awareness of the time when we shall have weathered the storms of life.

"But without faith it is impossible to please him: for he that cometh to God must believe that He is, and that He is a rewarder of them that diligently seek Him." Hebrews 11:6.

The Abundant Life: Its Prerequisite (Faith)

CHAPTER 6 The Abundant Life: The Holy Spirit in the Believer's Life

" For we walk by faith, not by sight" 2nd Cor. 5:7. "And I will pray the Father, and he shall give you another Comforter, that he may abide with you forever." John 14:16.

Christianity is one of the major world religions. While being similar in terms of having a Supreme Power, Christianity differs from all other religions in that it embodies a triune God; that Godhead is threefold: God the Father, God the Son, and God the Holy Spirit. This combined religious interfacing is generally known at the Trinity. Although The Abundant Life: The Holy Spirit in the Believer's Lifethe word <u>Trinity</u> does not appear in the Bible, there are –

The Abundant Life: Its Prerequisite (Faith)

nonetheless - numerous Scriptures that support this concept. Yet, many Bible reading individuals have difficulty in understanding the Holy Spirit as an integral part of the Trinity. Such persons can envision God as Creator and Jesus as the divine person who walked on this earth. But their envisioning capacity tends to be incapable of recognizing the Holy Spirit. Hence, they tend to downplay or neglect the Holy Spirit and His role in their frequently life. One of the most frequently used responses is to label the Holy Spirit as belonging to the Sanctified or Holy people. Well, friends, I have a somber message - we all need the Holy Spirit if we desire to live the abundant, consoling, and heavenly bound life. The writing, in this connection, is a teaching on the Holy Spirit; it has been entitled," The Holy Spirit in the Believer's Life." The study is planned to introduce us to the Holy Spirit; familiarize us with what Jesus taught about the Spirit in our life; and to identify three areas in which we have need of the Holy Spirit. Since the first objective is historical in origin, let us turn attention to an analysis of the Holy Spirit. In theology, the study of the Holy Spirit is known as Pneumatology. This is the area of study that seeks to define the origin, nature, and functioning of the Holy Spirit. A careful biblical analysis of the Holy Spirit discloses several historical facts, some of which are: the Holy Spirit was present at creation and (Gen. 1:2) records, "And the Spirit of God moved upon the face of the waters"; the Spirit was present at the creation of human life (Gen. 1:26) and therein it is recorded, "And God said, Let us make man in our image..."; the Spirit of God was present at the baptism of Jesus (Matt. 3:16) "... and he saw the Spirit of God descending like a dove, and lighting upon him..."; Jesus promised that the Holy Spirit, (Holy Ghost) would come upon the disciples (Acts 1:8) where it is recorded, "But ye shall receive power, after that the Holy Ghost is come upon you."; there was an outpouring of the Holy Spirit on the Day of Pentecost (Acts 2:4) where it is recorded, "And they were all filled with the Holy Ghost..." and the Spirit was with John on the Isle of Patmos (Rev. 1:9) where it is recorded, "I was in the Spirit on the Lord's day..."

Within a slightly different context, the Bible presents the Holy Spirit in terms of symbols that include: oil, water, wind, fire, a dove, a seal, and a pledge. Beloved, these are but a few of the numerous biblical references to the Holy Spirit.

The next consideration of the Holy Spirit is the Biblical division of the Godhead. Starting with Genesis and continuing throughout the Old Testament is the period where God is prominent; that period is known as God the Father. The second period starts with Matthew and continues through the 1st Chapter of Acts; it is the era where Jesus lived on this earth. That time is labeled as God the Son; during that time God was in the background while Jesus was at the forefront. The last component of the Godhead starts with Acts and ends with the Book of Revelation. It is the third part of the Godhead, known as God the Holy Spirit. This is the era under which we are living; it is characterized by God in the background of divinity, Jesus as the mediator next to God, and the Holy Spirit as the present force promised by Jesus. Beloved, this divine relation will prevail until the end of time, often referred to as the rapture. Our challenge, in this regard, is to prayerfully seek to learn of and allow the Holy Spirit to intervene in or life. Such an undertaking is consistent with the intent of Jesus as reflected in his message to the disciples as noted in our text; he said, "And I will pray the Father, and he shall give you another Comforter, that he may abide with you forever." (John 14:16).

Let us now turn to the second topic of the study; it is that of what Jesus taught about the Spirit in our life. In his commentary on this topic, Schofield wrote that "Christ indicates a threefold personal relationship of the Spirit to the believers: that relationship consists of three words; they are: "with" "in" and "upon". The key Scriptural references for these words are: John 14:17; Luke 24:49; and Acts 1:8). the Spirit The word, "with" indicates the approach of the Spirit to the soul; it is that of imparting faith, convicting of sin, presenting Christ as the object of faith, and regeneration. The next word, "in" describes the abiding presence of the Spirit in the believer's body, the capacity to give victory over the flesh, to create the

The Abundant Life: Its Prerequisite (Faith)

Christian character, to bear personal infirmities, to open a pathway to God's mercies, to maintain trust in God, and to experience the eternal warmth of divine presence. The last word, "upon" describes the outpouring of the Holy Spirit. This process is like rain falling on dry soil; it saturates the soil, relieves the soil's dryness, and increases the soil's productiveness. This upon function causes behavioral responses in the believer's life; it may be crying, witnessing, or helping the less fortunate. In sum, the with, in, and upon functions help to make the believer become a new creature in Christ Jesus.

Let us now turn to the third teaching on the Holy Spirit in the believer's life; it is the question of what, specific duties does the Holy Spirit perform in the believer's life. The Bible contains an extensive list; however, this writing will be confined to just three functions of Holy Spirit in the believer's life. First, the Holy Spirit will guide the believer into all truth. This promise is found in John 16:13 where it is recorded, "Howbeit when he, the Spirit of truth is come, he will guide you into all truth..." Friends, life is like a vacationing tourist who desires to visit high profiled locations in the city. Accordingly, the vacationer takes a tour bus or a trolley on which both operators give a narration as the trip proceeds.   In   most   instances,   the operators follow the script; however, there are some who become fascinated by the   crowd   and   begin   to   stretch   the extremities   of   truth.   In   a   stage   of excitement, the vacationer is prone to believe the tour guide's account. Well, the Holy Spirit is a tour guide for daily life. This guide, according to the Bible, is truthful and will guide all believers into the truth (John 16:13). Whereas the bus tour guide may comment on worldly truth and even some, scientific truth, the Holy Spirit goes beyond those types and concentrates on the spiritual truth. This type of truth can not be taught in school; instead, it requires intervention of the Holy Spirit. This spiritual truth, while existing in daily affairs, rises above text book principles and teacher speculation; it ascends to the ultimate source of wisdom - the type that cometh from the Father. In this regard, it is possible for one to be intellectually wise and spiritually unwise. Hence, it becomes necessary for the believer to constantly seek guidance of the Holy Spirit.

The next function of the Holy Spirit in the believer's life is that of teacher. This function was specified by Jesus as recorded in John 14:26 when he said, "But the Comforter, which is the Holy Ghost, whom the Father will send in my name, he shall teach you all things, and bring all things to your remembrance, what so ever I have said unto you." During a life time, each person is exposed to the teaching of numerous individuals. In general, the teaching contents are geared toward family life and educational goals.

The Abundant Life: Its Prerequisite (Faith)

CHAPTER 7 The Abundant Life: Its Barriers (# 1) The Broken Things of Life

"The God of all grace, after you have suffered a little while, shall himself make you perfect" 1st Peter 5:10

For many children, Christmas was a day of excitement and near ecstasy over the many toys and presents they received. Many of the boys, probably, being moved by curiosity busied themselves in examining, taking a part and trying to reassemble their toys. In some instances, they were successful, but there were numerous instances in which they were unsuccessful. In fact, some of them even broke their toys. Accordingly, many parents heard the distressful cry, "I broke my toy can you fix it for me?" In some instances, the answer was "yes"; however, there were situations in which the answer was "no". As would be expected grief followed.

Beloved, life contains a series of similar experiences for the whole of humanity. The elderly, the middle aged, the young adults, the adolescents, and the children - all have some experiences with broken things. Some individuals are capable of accepting the fact that something is broken; some persons become distressed as a result of broken things; some people hold others responsible for their broken things; and a few individuals seek, if at all possible, to find a fixer for broken things.

The writing, in this connection, will address the problem of broken things; it has been entitled, "The Broken Things of Life". It will examine two aspects of broken things of life: 1) What are some things that can be broken in life; 2) Does God intervene when we experience broken things in life?

Let us address the first concern that is what are some things that can be broken? It is herein submitted that there are three areas in which things can be broken. There are first the mechanical things: toys, automobiles, appliances, televisions, and computers. Many of the mechanical things have a warranty to partially cover the cost of repairs. The mechanical things can be carried to repair shops such as a garage, repair shops, and factor refurbishing facilities.

Secondly, there is the family that can be broken. The most pervasive break in the family is caused by death. That reality leaves a void in the household. The family as a broken unit causes prolonged grief and extensive loneliness. Family sociologists and clinical psychologists report that elderly couples, married for over 50 years, tend to experience unbearable grief. Hence, the survivor soon follows the deceased spouse.

Thirdly, the employment area is one in which we can find the broken things. Without sounding too political, the past few years have been a period of broken things in terms of employment. Homes have been lost, cars have been repossessed, credit cards have been lost, family abuse has increased, and personal confidence is at an all time low.   In this connection, references to a rebounding economy mean absolutely nothing to most people who are experiencing the broken thing of employment.

Friends, while these are but a few of the many broken things life, there is a more disturbing one; it is that of a broken relationship with Jesus as Lord and Savior. This fact leads to the second - and final - consideration of the writing; it is the question as to whether God intervenes when we have broken things in life? Beloved, our Bible tells us that God knows us; God cares for us; and God is ready to help us.   The text is but one reference to the ever presence and concern that God has for each of us.   Listen, again, to the words of Peter - "The God of all grace, after you have 5:10). Suffered a little while, shall himself make you perfect"(1st Peter).

Let us look a bit closer to Peter's statement about being made perfect. In the Greek text, the word "mend" is used. It was a term that the fishermen knew and used as they prepared holes in the fishing net. Those persons were familiar with the value of a net to catch the fish; hence, they spent time mending the net. In a similar manner, Peter is today reminding us that God is ready to mend our spiritual mind set. He may not repair a toy, but he will help you mind to things about something else

In closing, friends, The God of all grace shall mend our poor, broken, labor-worn lives - marred sometimes by our own failures, bruised and torn often by roughness of people in our lives. Heartbreaking and emotionally draining may be our experiences as we strive to uphold the faith, but let us never throw in the towel. Instead, let us examine the Bible for examples of people whose lives were mended after having experiences some broken things in life. The conversion of Saul on the Damascus Road is a lucid example of spiritual mending. (Acts 9). Prior to his experience on the Damascus, Saul was a prominent, highly educated, vocationally skilled tent maker, of both Jewish and Roman citizenship, and an ardent persecutor of Christians. He was present at the stoning of Stephen (Acts 7:58) and was so pleased with the incident that he chose to round up additional Christians. Accordingly, Saul

The Abundant Life: Its Barriers

obtained permission to visit Damascus for
the purpose of bounding Christians, men
and women, and bringing them back to
Jerusalem for persecution. Beloved, in
lay terminology, "his thing" was to be
recognized as a successful persecutor of
Christians. Unknown to or not
recognized by Paul was the existence of a
power greater than the source from which
he had received his order. He
experienced that Divine Power on the
Damascus Road. Thereon, according to
the Bible, a bright light shine on Saul, he
fell to the earth, and heard a voice saying,
" Saul, Saul, why persecutest thou me?"
(Acts9:4). Beloved, that event was
broken thing in Saul's life. It could not
be repaid by human mandates; instead,
the mending required the touch of the
Master's hand as symbolized by Ananias'

baptism of Saul.   Friends, the rest is Biblical history in which is noted that Saul (now Paul) became a prolific writer of epistles found in the New Testament, founder of Churches in the Gentile World, and mentor of young Christian leaders.

Beloved, life for us can so easily present "broken things" on our pathway. These broken things are in the family, on the job, in the community, financial resources, and physical health.   Unlike Saul whose objective was the source of his broken thing, ours can occur without evil purposes.   Within this context, we must never become bitter and withdrawn as we strive toward The Abundant Life. Instead, let us heed the admonition of Peter's message, "The God of all grace, after you have suffered a little while, shall himself make you perfect." (I Peter 5:10)

The Abundant Life: Its Barriers

At that glorious time you will recognize your entrance to The Abundant Life.

The Abundant Life: Its Barriers (#2) Facing the Disappointments in Life

"We are troubled on every side, yet not distressed; we are perplexed, but not in despair; persecuted, but not forsaken; cast down, but not destroyed" II Cor. 4:8-9.

Life is a short journey between birth and death. It is filled with diversified experiences. For many of us, life seems to be a continuous struggle amidst goals. There are others of us, however, who seem to be insulated from disappointments. Between these two extremities, the whole of humanity can be located.

The Abundant Life: Its Barriers

Throughout religious history there has been the recurring thought that righteous people are spared the agony of disappointments and suffering. Religion, in the regard, was viewed as a fence within which the righteous persons would be protected by God. However, a careful study of the Bible shows no support for the belief that being righteous is a safeguard against toils and tribulation.

There are numerous righteous personalities in the Old Testament and the New Testament who experienced disappointments and suffering. Job epitomized the Old Testament; he was a perfect and upright man who loved God and hated evil. Satan was aware of Job's righteousness and he challenged God to let him have access to Job. The account is well known of how Job suffered, but not without God's knowledge and care. The episode ended with Job overcoming the illness and becoming more prosperous than before.

Saint Paul is the New Testament person who experienced prolonged suffering and disappointment in his service for the Master. The Book of Acts gives a detailed account of his conversion, baptism, and early church minis He became a great preacher, a prolific writer, the first missionary to the Gentile World, and the builder of churches. His lofty accomplishments were not attained on flowery beds of ease; rather they were achieved as he struggled with adversaries, illnesses, magistrates, and physical torture.

Since Paul is the great theologian for Christianity and many of his doctrines form the core of both our belief and hope, the writing today will explore one aspect of his method for coping with the disappointments in life. The intent is to help us gleam insights for our use as we move from day to day. Ideally, we would like to experience happiness and satisfaction from day to day. Unfortunately, the real life situation is quite different. It is one of ups and downs. Often life seems to be filled with unpredictable events and insensitive persons. One writer has characterized life as "the best of times and the worst of times". Our concern, in this connection, is to find an effective way to cope with the worst of times. Since disappointments are prominent in the worst of time, we need a reliable method to handle them. Our writing, entitled Facing the

The Abundant Life: Its Barriers

Disappointments in Life will submit Saint Paul's message to the Corinthians as a model to cope with the disappointments in life.

The Pauline approach to disappointments no blessed prayer cloth; it is no affirmation ritual, and it is no horoscope reading. It is, rather, a rational acknowledgment that life does have disappointments and sufferings. But Saint Paul reminds us that we live, move, and have our being under a God who knows and loves us. Further, he tells us that our God allowed his Son, Jesus, to take a human body and live for 33 years among people who would experience much suffering and disappointment for Him. Jesus, in full knowledge of these realities, nonetheless called upon the believers to be "faithful unto death and He will give them a crown of life." (Rev.   2:10).

Saint Paul accepted the teaching about the crown of life and shortly before he was beheaded in Rome, he wrote to Timothy and made reference to being ready for his crown (2nd Timothy 4:8). He, also, said that a crown of life awaited everyone who loved the Lord and awaited his coming.

Our question today is - how can we position ourselves to received crown of life while living in a world of disappointments and suffering? The answer is contained in Paul's second letter to the Corinthians.   In verses 8 and 9 of that chapter, Paul identifies four life experiences that are disappointing and heartbreaking.   Each type continues to be a part of the human experiences.   In order that we may know them, attention will now be directed to each one.

Trouble - The word trouble is unpleasant both in sound and implication. It refers to a disturbance, an agitation, a discomfort, a misfortune, and a pain. Trouble is viewed as an uninvited guest who is always like a pest waiting to invade the human experience. Trouble is also associated with suffering both physical and psychological. It seems to linger around those who are committed to ethics, fair play, and Christian values. It was in this regard that Jesus told the disciples that in this world they would have tribulations, and they did. In responding to that situation, Saint Paul wrote, "We are troubled on every side, yet we are not distressed." (2nd Corinthians 4:8). What a statement of both faith and determination - troubled on every side, but not distressed. What was their secret weapon? It could well have been their knowledge that they were more than conquerors through Christ who strengthened them.

Perplexed - The second life experience contained in the text is that of being perplexed. This word refers to being filled with uncertainty, to be confused, or bewildered. The Saint Paul was talking about their daily experiences of being uncertain as to what the new day would bring. He and his fellow travelers were concerned about their safety, their food, and their next opposition. They were fully aware of the general animosity toward them and the dislike for their preaching. While recognizing the dangerous environment in which they were preaching, Paul declared that they were "...not in despair" (2nd Corinthians 4:8). It seems that his message was that even in their greatest perplexities, they knew that God was forever with them and He would protect them from hurt, harm, and danger. Their unequivocal trust in God sends a message to us today. Essentially, it is enshrined in the words, "I'll trust in God, though come what may."

Persecuted - The third disappointing experience is that of being persecuted. This word denotes an act designed to afflict, injure, or cause mental agony. It is, further, a type of annoyance and it may come as a result of one's religion, politics, ethnic origin, or ethical standards. Saint Paul, according to the Bible, was a victim of persecution although he had earlier been a persecutor (Acts 9). However in his new role as

The Abundant Life: Its Barriers

defender of the Gospel, Paul was persecuted by men in different places along his missionary journeys. His persecution came not from doing wrong; it was rather an expression of evil people trying to block the flow of righteousness.

Jesus knew that persecution was one consequence for those who followed Him; hence, He addressed that problem in His first sermon often referred to as the Beatitudes. Therein He said, "Blessed are ye, when men shall revile you, and persecute you, and shall say all manner of evil against you falsely, for my sake. Rejoice, and exceeding glad: for great is your reward in heaven: for so persecuted they the prophets which were before you" (Matthew 5:11-12). That Sermon on the Mount continues to beacon hope to all who love the Lord and await His coming.

Remember, "Good men may be sometimes forsaken of their friends, as well as persecuted by their enemies but God will never leave them nor forsake them".

Cast Down - The fourth, textually specified, disappointing experience is being cast down. To be cast down is the same as being discarded, subdued, and trampled over. Often in life, the adversary seems in great measure to prevail, and our spirits begin to fail us. Oh! there may be fear within and bodily trembling, but the child of God is, "...not destroyed" (2nd Corinthian 4:9) Our challenge, in this connection, is to, " life our eyes unto the hills from whence cometh our help" (Psalm 121:1). Beloved, we will experience attempts by the enemies of God to bring us down, to

The Abundant Life: Its Barriers

destroy our dreams, to subdue our faith, to ruin our lives, to divert us from the pathway of righteousness and to block us from The Abundant Life. In facing such disappointments, let us never forget Saint Paul's message to the Corinthians, "...cast down, but not destroyed..." (2nd Corinthian 4:9).

In closing, friends, whatever may be your problems, disappointments, or apparent failures in life, never forget that you are a creation of the Almighty God who knows and cares about your welfare. So in the reassuring words of Saint Paul, you can find comfort, motivation, and anticipation in your prayerful effort to experience The Abundant Life.

The Abundant Life: Its Barriers (#3) The Theology of Affliction

"Rejoice in the Lord always: and again I say, Rejoice" (Phil. 4:4) "Casting all your care upon him: for he careth for you" (1 Peter 5:7)

Approximately twenty-five years ago, the Institutional member ship was in the young adult category; it was vibrate, career oriented, inquisitive, gregarious, and upwardly mobile. Its offspring's, if any, were prenatal, in the cradle, or young children. The members were highly visible in social circles, agile on the dance floor -according to unsolicited reports - cautiously experimental in beverage diversity, vivid sport fans, and loyal to Greekdom. Yet this membership was impelled by an urge for spiritual enlighten, but under a credentialed leader. It became this founding pastor's divine opportunity to fill the void between academe and theology. Accordingly, Institutional - the young fellowship - commenced a sail that is yet afloat.

Since those golden years of infancy and development, the Institutional membership has undergone family bereavements, illnesses, hospitalizations, surgeries, chronic illness, and geriatric decrements. Added to these realities is that of primary care giving for parents, children, and spouses while attempting to fulfill occupational responsibilities.

Since the new health related demand can be overwhelming and

engender questions as to their origin, duration, and amelioration, the writing for today was planned to give a biblical explanation for and reactions to these health related problems. It has been prepared around the subject - The Theology of Affliction. It will address three dimension of affliction and/or suffering; namely, the historic concern as to the origin of physical suffering, some biblical teachings about affliction and, 3) a theological modality for coping with affliction.

Prior to an examination of these dimensions, attention will be placed on two concepts used in the subject. First is the word, "theology". Lewis Chafer, in his eight volume work entitled Systematic Theology, defined theology as the study of God: nature, functions, and duration. This word is a derivative of the Greek concept," Theos", a term that denotes God. Since God's message to humankind is recorded in the Bible, also known as the Auto Script, humanity is challenged to read, believe, and accept its teaching. The second word, affliction, is one of the dreaded realities of human existence. Affliction can be defined as a condition of physical malfunctioning. It causes pain, stress, worry, annoyance, embarrassment and even a decline in self-esteem.

Since human beings are hedonistic, i.e., preferring pleasure to pain, there is an ongoing effort to maintain good health as long as possible. While such goals are admirable, the fact is that afflictions are unpredictable and quite democratic. Hence, no one can foretell the encroachment of affliction to self or family members. When affliction, the unwelcome visitor, does come with an unspecified duration, the individual and family members are often baffled in terms of origin, treatments, duration, and post recovery prospects.   Within that baffling situation, there are thoughts and inquiries as to the afflictions.   Beloved, capitalistic society is quite aware of human desperation caused by afflictions; hence, it is filled with quasi remedies that include over the counter medications, on line medications, herbal specialists, "root doctors", psycho therapist, and physicians - to mention but a few of the so called helping professions.   While demeaning these sources, the writing today offers an effective method to anchor oneself for coping with afflictions.   It is lifted from the Holy Bible, and as Peter asserted, that message was "...written by Holy Men of

The Abundant Life: Its Barriers

Old as they were moved by the Holy Spirit." (II Peter 1:20-21). This fact leads now to the earlier defined consideration of the subject, the first of which is-the historic concern regarding the origin and nature of afflictions.

Among the first segment of questions in philosophy is that regarding the origin of affliction also known as evil. The biblical character, Job, constituted the focus of this inquiry. My students were asked to explain the suffering of Job from the medical, the philosophical, and the biblical points of view. Invariably, they said, medically, Job had contacted a virus; from the philosophical stance, Job was just a victim of circumstances, and from the biblical perspective, Job was being tried in accordance with God's will. Although these explanations have merit, the biblical one was a paradox for the philosopher, Epicurus. He argued that if God is all powerful, then why does he not prevent all forms of affliction. In contrast, if He can prevent then by allowing it to occur means that God is less than a compassionate being.

The Biblical view, in contrast with philosophy, traces the origin of affliction back to the Garden of Eden. Therein the first couple was created as perfect beings; it had the privilege of unbroken fellowship with God. Unfortunately, that prospect was short lived; it was broken with the transgression in the Garden. Accordingly, God expelled them from the Garden; the fellowship was broken and their immortal bodies became mortal. Hence, the whole of humanity inherited a less than perfect body. Thus, each person has the prospect of becoming afflicted owing to the Original Sin and not because of a personally committed transgression. It is, therefore, incorrect that an ill person, or a physically challenged person is being punished for some act earlier committed. Beloved, let us not get bogged down with these and other explanations; instead, may we remember that God is absolute, just, and righteous. Further, His will is sovereign, His power is unlimited, and his love is everlasting. Hence, God knows who we are, where we are, what we need, and just how much we can bear.

The fact that God is in control of everything, including afflictions, leads to the second consideration of this writing; it is that of biblical teachings on afflictions. Whenever this topic is studied biblically, three names surface one is Job who was perfect and upright, yet he endured prolonged suffering; amidst his suffering, Job said," Though he slays me yet will I trust him". The second person is Saint Paul who said of the thorn in his flesh, that he prayed three times for removal, but heard the Lord say, "My grace is sufficient". The third person who calls upon the believers to cast their cares upon Him by saying that God cares for you is Peter.

My friends, these three persons: Job, Paul, and Peter have left us a legacy for use when waves of affliction sweep over the soul. However, Saint Paul stands along in his writing on the subject; the reference letter is the Book of Philippians. Within the four chapters of that book can be found a modality for coping with affliction. This fact leads to the last consideration of this writing; it is that of a method to cope with suffering and affliction. The key to the method is found in Chapter 4, our text, where Saint Paul called upon the Philippians to "Rejoice in the Lord always, I will say again, rejoice". Writing on the difficulty of finding joy amidst affliction, Warren Wiersbe noted, "Worry, worry, worry! How many Christians lose their joy and peace because of worry?". He said that Paul felt that a secure mind is the sole requirement for peace in the midst of sorrows. But the secure mind, one that relies on God for everything, comes only after three other mind sets; they are the single mind (Chapter 1) thinking continually on Jesus; the submissive mind (Chapter 2) yielding to the will of God –

The Abundant Life: Its Barriers

Job; and the spiritual mind (Chapter 3) resting confidently underneath the Almighty God's canopy of love. Friends, once we shall have attained the secure mind, we can feel God's presence; we can experience his peace; we can share his power and we can enjoy his provision. With this secure mind, we can pray right and we can think right. Then, and only then, can we truthfully recognize the confident stance, "I can do all things through Christ which strengtheneth me." (Phil. 4:13). With this level of spiritual awareness, we can commence to think positively about our self under the canopy of the everlasting God whose joy is for us to experience The Abundant Life. Remember the saying of Jesus, the only begotten of the Father, "...I am come that they may have life, and have it more abundantly" (John 10:10).

CHAPTER 8 The Abundant Life: Its Foe
(Satan) Satan: His Purpose

Isaiah 14: 12 How art thou fallen from heaven, O Lucifer, son of the morning! How art thou cut down to the ground, which didst weaken the nations!

Three of the major world religions are Judaism, Christianity, and Islam. Each of these religions is based upon a sacred book. Judaism uses only the Old Testament of the Bible; Christianity is based upon both the Old and New Testaments and Islam, uses a different book known as the Holy Koran. Collectively, these religions are known as the Abrahamic Religions because they can be traced back to two sons of Abraham: Ishmael and Isaac.

Of particular interest for the writing today is the religion known as Christianity and its sacred book which is the Holy Bible. This book, The Holy Bible, is the inerrant, immutable, and eternal word of God. Although God was the author, Peter viewed man as the penman. Thus he wrote, "For the prophecy came not in old time by the will of man: but holy men of God spake as they were moved by the Holy Ghost." (II Peter 1:21).

The Bible gives a narration of the heavenly beings, the creation, and the start of human life, to mention but few of its accounts. In the script of this text is the origin of Satan. As noted in the text, Satan's original state was that of an angel whose name was Lucifer. Following the text, further, Lucifer is presented as an over ambitious angel who sought to become coequal with, if not superior to, God.

This rebellious act caused Lucifer to be cast out of heaven and become known as Satan. In his new position, Satan was known by a names that included deceiver, the devil, the evil one, prince of the air, and the father of lies.

The Bible contains a record of Satan's earthly activities since his fall. It has been and continues to be that of tempting humanity. His presence was evident in the Garden of Eden (Genesis 3:1-4; at the household of Job (Job 1:6-7); in the wilderness with Jesus (Matthew 4:1-11); and in the temple with Peter and Ananiah (Acts 5:1-6). In addition to these few biblical accounts of Satan's presence, it must be noted that he is yet on the move. However, the Christian believer's obligation is to resist the Satan. Accordingly, this sermon has been entitled, "Resisting the devil". It will be anchored by the following critical objections: 1.To alert us to the fact that the devil is a real spirit; 2. To enlighten us on some of the devil's tricks, and 3. To assure us that we can claim a victory over the devil.

Prior to addressing these objectives, attention will be focused on prevailing misconceptions about the devil. We are living during a time where there are many views, ideas, teachings, philosophies, and religious notions about the devil. As would be expected, people are scattered among all of these beliefs. Two of the more frightening of these beliefs are: (a) a religion that teaches the absence of good and evil; it claims that thought is the ultimate power and, therefore, a person can erase evil by merely thinking good thoughts; the other extreme view is a practice known as Satanism in which people actually worship the devil as do Christians worship God.

The popularity of Satanic worship is causing widespread social problems such as cultism, murder of animals and human sacrifices in devil worship ceremonies. In the meantime, the Christian band has responded as nervous captives while hearing about the spread of evil actions. Many Christians are installing security systems, obtaining licenses to carry firearms, and purchasing other gadgets to defend themselves against workers of iniquity. While all of these efforts are commendable and they do offer some feeling of security, we - Christians - must never forget the power and authority of prayer to resist the devil. We should, further, remember that Jesus came not only to reunite the broken chain between God and humanity, but to withstand the devil and leave us with knowledge and power to resist the devil.

Against this background of views on the devil, the first focus will now shift to the three critical objectives earlier mentioned, the first of which is -

1. The devil is a real Spirit - The existence of devil is recorded in many Books of the Bible. He appears in various episodes from Genesis (3: 1) to Revelation (20:10). The Bible has numerous references to Satan as being a real spirit. It tells us that Satan was part

of the original creation; he was an angel whose name was Lucifer. Ezekiel described him as having beautiful jeweled clothing and possessing a robust body form along with a sharp mind (Ezek. 28). Ezekiel also tells us that Satan was ambitious and attempted, in vain, to challenge God's power. Accordingly, Satan recruited other angels to help him defeat God. Obviously, he failed and, for his plot, Satan and his followers were thrown out of Heaven. He was, however, allowed to have power to disrupt events and people on earth. In this capacity, Satan became known as the prince of the air and the father of lies.

Satan first appeared in the Garden of Eden; there he tempted Eve to disregard God's order to avoid eating fruit from the tree which is in the midst of the garden (Genesis 3:3). He said unto her, "Ye shall not surely die" (Genesis 3:4). Eve yielded to Satan's temptation and became the first human to sin against God. From that triumph of Eve, Satan commenced his perpetual journey in search for more victims. He caused Moses to smote the rock; David to cohabit with Bethsheba; Saul to pursue David; Absalom to plot against David and Satan was present in Job's household when his family came together.

Satan's rampage encountered an obstacle when he sought to attempt Jesus after his baptism (Matthew 4:1-11) He appealed to the hunger, vanity, and pride of Jesus. Each of the temptations was countered with reference to the Scriptures. So Satan was unsuccessful in his attempt to tempt Jesus, but he is yet active in his earthly purpose of tempting people to The devil has many tricks - Satan, often called the devil, has specific methods to cause our downfall. His methods never change; they are the same as he used on Eve and later Ananias. They are two in number:

1.   Satan seeks to contradict God's laws. Remember, he said to Eve, "ye shall not surely die... shall be as gods (Gen.   3:3-4). Sadly, Eve yielded to Satan's temptation and she influenced her husband, Adam, to join in the transgression. God was dissatisfied with their action so He expelled them from the Garden of Eden (Genesis 3:23-24). Beloved, they had fallen to one of Satan's tricks - i.e., lies.

Satan's next trick is that of appealing to human vanity.   He reminds us of our special features: appearance, intellect, possessions, positions, and clothing. He makes us feel that no one can measure up to us; he tells us that we are special and we must see ourselves above all others. In yielding to this temptation, we become members of Satan's host. He is happy, God is grieved, and our integrity is blemished. Friends, we can avoid falling into the grip of Satan by merely reading and embracing the teaching of Proverbs 16:18; it states, "Pride goeth before destruction and a haughty spirit before a fall." The prospect of preventing this fall leads to the final consideration of the writing; it is the fact that:

1. The devil can be defeated. Although the devil, or Satan, has troubled people throughout the annals of time, he

can be defeated. Our Savior was the first person to defeat Satan. The Bible records this event in the 4th Chapter of Matthew. Some may argue that we are imperfect whereas Jesus was perfect; therefore, we are unable to resist the devil. Beloved, that type of reasoning is incorrect because the Bible has a plan for us to resist the devil. It is found in the 1st Peter 5:7-10. Within those verses, Peter gives us three principles for resisting the devil. Let us look at them. First, he calls on us to be sober. This requirement is not confined to drinking or drugs; rather, it includes common sense in daily affairs. Sobriety, also, denotes letting the mind rule over the heart. Next, Peter tells us to be steadfast. This requirement denotes the act of standing firmly for right and righteousness and knowing that our adversary, the devil, as a roaring lion, walketh about, seeking whom he may devour (1St Peter 5:8).

Finally, Peter tells us that the devil can be resisted through prayer. Moreover, he reminds us that the devil is our adversary and he, "as a roaring lion, walketh about seeking whom he may devour." (1st Peter 5:8). Satan's presence in the gathering of Job's family clearly shows his roaming nature. Saint Paul was fully aware of the cunning tactics of Satan and he, therefore called upon the Corinthians to be ever mindful of this deceiver and avoid letting him get the advantage over them (2nd Cor. 2:11). Our response, in this connection, must be that of confronting the devil with the Word of God and prayer. Remember, Jesus used the Word of God in response to the three temptations Satan sought to use on him in the wilderness. (Matthew 4: 1-11). That glorious fact reminds us that the Devil can be resisted through prayer. Our challenge, in facing Satan, is to humble ourselves "...therefore under the mighty hand of God, that he may exalt us in due time." (1St Peter 5:6). This Scripture and many others assure us that Satan can be resisted through prayer.

In closing, let us remember that Satan is a chief fallen angel; he has innumerable angelic and human followers. Satan is the great tempter. He causes humankind to be envious, hostile, disenchanted, and angry with self and others. He plants seeds of dissatisfaction with self and dislike for others, especially those who seem to be happy, successful, and experiencing the

The Abundant Life: Its Foe (Satan)

abundant life. Beloved such disgruntled persons can turn their life around through reading and believing the Word of God, commencing a regular prayer life, and thanking God for their daily bread.   Once this type of mind set has taken root in the subconscious, the believer will have resisted Satan, obtained a new outlook on life, and be on the pathway to The Abundant Life.

CHAPTER 9The Abundant Life: Its Culmination The End of Time *Revelation 4:1*

Time is a topic of historic interest. In general, it is viewed between two polarities, of extremes - the beginning and the ending. Time is a standard for measurements that include age, longevity on a job, duration of marriage, years of formal training, and days of vacation.

Time has numerous implications, some of which are: physiological; educational; economical; materialistic and the certainty that all will one day pass away.

While all of these time related

The Abundant Life: Its Culmination

terms are important, it seems tenable to conclude the morality is ultimately the time anchored reality that concerns humanity. Within this context, the Holy Bible speaks to this human concern. It tells us, for example, that time started with God as noted in Genesis 1:1 "In the beginning God created the heaven and the earth". The Bible, also, informs us that time will at some point come to an end. This certainly was revealed to John on the Island of Patmos; it is the basis of our text today. The words are..."Come up hither, and I will shew thee things which must be hearafter" (Rev. 4:1). This Scripture along with Genesis 1, certifies to us that God is the source of time; He started it, He is sustaining it, and He will end it!. This writing, in this connection, has been entitled," The End of

The Abundant Life: Its Culmination

Time". It has no intention of frightening us or making any predictions as to when it shall occur; the intent, rather, is to alert us to this ultimate reality.

This writing is couched in the following objectives: 1) to alert us to the Biblical certainty that time will one day come to an end, 2) to familiarize us with events signifying the impending end of time, and 3) to remind us of how to prepare for the end of time. Prior to addressing these objectives, attention will be focused on the Book of Revelation. This book is one of five written by Saint John the Divine. Those books include: The Gospel of John, the 1st, 2nd, and 3rd Epistles of John, and the book of Revelation. This last book of John was written while he was banished to the Island of Patmos. He had been ordered there by Emperor Domitian who found John's teaching a threat to his title as emperor and lord of Rome. John had boldly rejected the emperor's claim and preached, rather, that Christ is Lord and King. In response, the Emperor had John carried to the Island of Patmos. He was successful in separating John from the Christians, but he was unable to block the flow of divine revelation. Thus, John was banned from Rome but on that lonely Island of Patmos, his spiritual cup was filled with divine revelation that included a glimpse of the end of time.

Against this background on the book of Revelation, let us now turn to the objectives earlier identified, the first of which is - *the certainty that time will one day come to an end.* The Bible has numerous teachings about the end of time. That ultimate reality was of concern to the disciples; hence, they inquired of Jesus as to when the end would come. Jesus addressed that question in the 24th Chapter of Matthew and He told he disciples to "Watch there fore: for ye know not what hour your Lord doth come"(24:42).

In general, the Biblical writers, except Saint John, seemed to avoid a section on the end of time. Hence, it was left to Saint John to pen the account of that unavoidable event. It is recorded in the Book of Revelation. That book, in theological circles, is known as apocalyptic - a word that denotes a view of the future. The writing from that Book cites John's testimony as to an experience he had, when he was in the spirit on the Lord's day. He tells us that the door was opened in heaven, he heard a voice as if a trumpet talking saying unto him - "Come up hither, and I will shew thee things that must come". (Rev 4:1). His apocalyptic view included: four beast, twenty elders, seven angels, a pale horse, a white horse, a black horse, and a red horse; 144 thousand redeemed, and a seal that no one able to break. John's narrative continues with the cry who is worthy to break the seal; he noted that the elders found none to be worthy. Much to their surprise, there appeared one riding the white horse and radiating such light that the elders cried aloud," Worthy is the Lamb of God who has broken the seal". But between that event and the end of time would come additional events that John saw. He noted the fall of Babylon (Chapter 17) an event that will be referenced later in this writing. Additionally, John wrote about the thousand years reign of Satan and the final battle with Christ being victorious. Afterward, John tells us that Christ would reign as King of King and Lord of Lords. Beloved he described that event as the new heaven and the new earth.

Let us now turn to the second objective which is that of identifying signs of the end of time. The Bible talks about how difficult it is to distinguish between winter and summer - that situation is becoming more evident. It talks about immorality becoming more evident. This situation is being popularized on TV, movies, and places of sexual perversions. The Bible also describes, in Revelation, the beginning of a final struggle between the East and West with a Western leader emerging as an Anti Christ. He will declare his mission is to purge the world of an Eastern threat. The Bible depicts that impending confrontation as the Battle of Armageddon. Without becoming political, attention is called to the political claim of rooting out terrorism. Beloved, our nation has a history of terrorism. It terrorized the American Indians; it terrorized of terrorism. It terrorized the American Indians; it terrorized the Slaves; it terrorized the emancipated Blacks; it terrorized the Chinese labors on the Union Pacific Railroad; and it is now terrorizing illegal immigrants through exploitative tactics. Does not the Bible teach that charity begins at home and spreads abroad. This assessment is not designed to instill fear; rather, it seeks to highlight some biblical prophecies concerning the end of time. Lastly, the question becomes how should we prepare ourselves for <u>The End of Time?</u> In pondering this question, each person must respond on two different levels, namely the worldly and the spiritual. The worldly consideration include mending broken fences in human relationships, drafting an end of life medical document, making pre-need funeral arrangements, and preparing a will for the legal and orderly transfer of one's earlier attainments in The Abundant Life.

The second level of action in preparation for the end of life is the spiritual arena. From the Christian perspective, it is highly desirable that the believer will have accepted Jesus as Lord and Savior along with a commitment to serve him throughout life. This act aligns the believer for the heavenly reward as promised in Revelation 2:10. "Be thou faithful unto death and I will give thee a crown of life". Admittedly, many individuals will have passed before the ultimate end of time. Yet all believers should not feel neglected with respect to the return of Jesus. Instead every saved person should embrace the message as recorded in the First Thessalonians 4:16-17. "For the Lord himself shall descend from heaven with a shout, with the voice of the archangel, and the dead in Christ shall rise first. Then we which are alive and remain shall be caught up with them in the clouds, to meet the Lord in the air: and so shall ever be with the Lord." Our second consolation, in preparing for the end of time, is found in the First Epistle of John, Chapter 3:2 "Beloved, now are sons of God, and it doth not yet appear what we shall be: but we know that when he shall appear, we shall be like him, for we shall see him as he is". Finally, a somber warning is given in Revelation 20:12 where it is shown that no one can avoid the responsibility of standing before the throne of God at which time the dead will be judged and whosoever name is not found in the book of life will be cast into the lake of fire" (15).

So in closing, beloved, while pursuing The Abundant Life, please be ever mindful of the transitory nature of life. In this regard, there are two unalterable facts - one a statement and the other a question; they are: "Soon death shall come and rob us all of what

The Abundant Life: Its Culmination

we here possess", and the other is a question - "For what shall it profit a man if he shall gain the whole world and lose his own soul?" (Mark 8:36).

CHAPTER 10

Epilogue

Life starts without the baby having any knowledge of material possessions. Within the ongoing socialization process, the child is exposed to worldly objects. Soon a desire for ownership emerges and it becomes increasingly evident as the individual moves into the adolescent stage. Because of various factors, however, not everyone has ready access to the use and/or ownership of material possessions. Yet the "Spirit of American Capitalism" extols the values of private ownership.

The focus on material gains causes widespread efforts to share in fruits of capitalism.   However, the fact remains that there is a differential access to <u>The Abundant Life.</u>   Yet there is the continuous desire to share in the nation's wealth.   The luster of material access causes many dreams, various efforts, and numerous doubts..   On the unfortunate side, this desire leads many into the arena of illegal activities.

In an effort to provide a socially approved and Christian anchored approach for a "comfort zone" in the struggle for material access, this book entitled, <u>The Abundant Life,</u> was written. It contains no magic scheme for becoming rich, nor does it make claims that every reader will experience abundance in the economic sphere.   It does assert, however, that the serious reader will find a practical approach for living <u>The Abundant Life,</u>

As indicated in the Preface, this book was written to present biblically anchored guidelines for experiencing The Abundant Life.   The guidelines are conveyed through a series of scripts, each of which embodies a teaching on the Abundant Life. The writing were presented under nine (9) different headings or chapters, each of which focused on some aspect of The Abundant Life. Chapter 1 - traced the origin of abundance to God,

Chapter 2 - identified the Bible as the reference for abundance

Chapter 3 - depicted Jesus as the access to abundance

Chapter 4 - presented prayer as the thrust to abundance,

Chapter 5 - specified faith as the prerequisite for abundance

Chapter 6 - showed that believers are the recipients of abundance

Chapter 7 - delineated barriers to abundance

Chapter 8 - labeled Satan as the foe to abundance

Chapter 9 - submitted death as the culmination of abundance.

In closing, this book has offered a

biblically based method for believers to attain The Abundant Life. It made no claims as to when the change will occur not does it guarantee a specific level of abundance. In regard to quantity of abundance, the reader is reminded of t he biblical fact involving talents. That account showed that people differ in their number and types of talents. This same divine principle applies to the economic aspects of life. Some people will be blessed with wealth, some with high income jobs, some with minimum wages, some with welfare checks, and some without any dependable source of income. Admittedly, these financial differences can cause envy and - in extreme cases - desperation. To provide guidance in coping with financial disparities regardless of one's level, this book on The Abundant Life was written.

Hopefully, it will provide direction, comfort, and inspiration for the reader in search of The Abundant Life.

The Biblical Base: A Justification

All professions and trades have established manuals upon which areas are based and for use in implementing the respective practice. A standard document in medical practice is <u>The Physician's Reference Manual.</u> In clinical psychology the standard manual for diagnosis is the <u>DSM-III.</u> In theology, it is <u>Chafer's Systematic Theology.</u> For Lexicon references, it is <u>Webster's Collegiate Dictionary</u>, and for the Judeo-Christian guidelines to pursue the abundant life, it is <u>The Bible (KJV)</u> from which all biblical references were lifted for us in this book on The Abundant Life.

Bibliography

The Physician's Reference Book
Copyright 2010, PDR Network
ISBN 1563637504

Chafer's Systematic Theology
Copyright 1993 Kregel Academic &
Professional
ISBN 978-0825423406

**Webster Collegiate Dictionary 10th
Edition**
Copyright 2007, Merriam Webster
ISBN 978-0877797081

The Bible (KJV)
Copyright 2000, Zondervan Publishing
Library of Congress Card Number
99-75836

www.ingramcontent.com/pod-product-compliance
Lightning Source LLC
Chambersburg PA
CBHW031849090426
42741CB00005B/409